STUDY GUIDE

What Is Reformed Theology?

R.C. Sproul

LIGONIER MINISTRIES
Renew your Mind.

LIGONIER.ORG | 800.435.4343

Copyright © 1999, 2010 Ligonier Ministries
421 Ligonier Court, Sanford, FL 32771
E-mail: info@ligonier.org
All rights reserved.
No reproduction of this work without permission.
Printed in the United States of America.

An Introduction by R.C. Sproul

The Protestant church is under assault more than ever to give up the biblical distinctives that made the Reformation a necessity. Unfortunately, most evangelicals don't know when the Reformation occurred, don't know what it was about, and don't understand the debt they owe men such as Martin Luther and John Calvin. So the question "What is Reformed theology?" has become a critical question in my lifetime, not a mere marketing-savvy title to grab your attention.

We realize that God has brought Ligonier Ministries in contact with Christians from many different backgrounds, particularly since the addition of our radio ministry in 1994. Thus, we created a series that would introduce people to the basics of Reformed theology. This study guide is part of that series known as, *What Is Reformed Theology?*

My hope is that we can help you understand that the question "What is Reformed theology?" is virtually the same as asking "How do I know and love the God of the Bible?" This is no platonic platitude we are exploring, but the very heart of God's revelation to us. With that in mind, I hope this study guide will aid you as you work to understand the heights and depths of the God who has spoken to us in His Word.

Sincerely,

R.C. Sproul

1

Introduction

MESSAGE OVERVIEW

I. Introduction
   a. Several years ago, David Wells wrote a book titled *No Place for Truth*, in which he outlined his concern over the demise of confessional theology in the evangelical church.
   b. The Alliance of Confessing Evangelicals was formed to call the evangelical church back to its confessional foundation.
   c. The purpose of this series to to provide an overview of the essence of Reformed theology.
II. Reformed Theology is a Theology
   a. There is a significant difference between religion and theology.
   b. The difference is seen in the two major approaches to questions of faith.
      i. In the God-centered approach, anthropology (the study of man) is subsumed under theology (the study of God).
      ii. In the man-centered approach, religion is studied as a sub-category of anthropology.
   c. Theology is the study of God.
   d. Religion is the study of types of human behavior.
III. Reformed Theology is a Belief System with God at its Center
   a. In Exodus 32:17ff, we read of men who had theology, but it was a corrupt one that led them to worship the creature rather than the Creator.
   b. Man's most basic sin is idolatry.
   c. Even the Christian religion can become idolatrous if we place at the center of our worship something other than God Himself.
   d. The most strict focus of Reformed theology is upon the knowledge of the true God.
   e. Theology is life because theology is the knowledge of God.

STUDY QUESTIONS

1. Is there a difference between theology and religion?

2. What are the two major approaches to questions of faith?

3. What is the basic meaning of theology?

4. What is the basic meaning of religion?

5. What is man's most basic sin?

DISCUSSION QUESTIONS

1. Has there been a demise of confessional theology in the twentieth century evangelical church? What are some of the possible reasons for our current situation? Discuss your answers.

2. What are some ways Christian worship can and has become idolatrous?

FURTHER STUDY

Sproul, R.C. *Grace Unknown*, pp. 9-20
Sproul, R.C. *Essential Truths of the Christian Faith*
Sproul, R.C. *Dust to Glory: An Overview of the Bible with R.C. Sproul*
Sproul, R.C. *Faith Alone*
Sproul, R.C. *Foundations: An Overview of Systematic Theology with R.C. Sproul*
Alliance of Confessing Evangelicals (www.alliancenet.org)
Gerstner, John. *Westminster Confession of Faith*
Wells, David. *No Place for Truth*

2

Evangelical, Catholic, & Reformed

MESSAGE OVERVIEW

I. Reformed Theology is a Systematic Theology
   a. Historically, the task of systematic theology has been to listen to the details of the Bible and discern how all of its truths fit together.
   b. The primary assumption of systematic theology is that the Bible is coherent.
   c. Every doctrine of Christianity touches every other doctrine in some way.
   d. The whole of Christian faith is intimately and intricately related.
II. Reformed Theology Involves an Apparent Paradox
   a. There is nothing particularly distinctive in what Reformed confessions teach regarding theology proper (the doctrine of God).
   b. But the most distinctive feature of Reformed theology is its doctrine of God.
   c. All Christians have a basically orthodox creedal affirmation regarding the doctrine of God, but to many it is one doctrine among many, rather than the controlling doctrine.
III. Reformed Theology is Catholic
   a. The Reformation of the sixteenth century was an attempt to recover the apostolic faith.
   b. Reformed theology continues to embrace the catholic truths that all Christians affirm.
   c. In this sense, Reformed theology may be said to be "catholic," which means universal.
   d. These common, core doctrines are the foundation upon which the others rest.
   e. There is a tendency to think of Reformed theology only in terms of its distinctives, but the distinctives rest upon a common foundation shared with a host of other Christian bodies.
IV. Reformed Theology is Evangelical
   a. All who are evangelical are catholic, but not all who are catholic are evangelical.

- b. Similarly, all Reformed Christians are evangelical, but not all evangelicals are Reformed.
- c. Reformed theology shares a common evangelical heritage with its Protestant brothers.
- d. The Reformers believed that with the proclamation of justification by faith alone they were recovering the evangel.
- e. Protestants used the word *evangelical* to say that they embraced Martin Luther's view of *sola fide*.

V. Reformed Theology is Reformed
- a. The term "Reformed" is a further distinctive sub-classification.
- b. A Reformed doctrine is one that is specific to the Reformed faith and is not held by all evangelicals.

STUDY QUESTIONS

1. What is the task of systematic theology? What is its fundamental assumption?

2. What is the apparent paradox regarding Reformed theology and its doctrine of God? Why is the paradox not real?

3. What do we mean when we say that Reformed theology is "catholic"?

4. What do we mean when we say that Reformed theology is "evangelical"?

5. What were the Reformers trying to communicate by their use of the term *evangelical* as a self-designation?

6. What is meant by the use of the term "Reformed"?

DISCUSSION QUESTIONS

1. Discuss the reasons why it is vitally important that our theology remain catholic in the true sense of the word.

2. What is the relationship between the core catholic doctrines, the specifically evangelical doctrines, and the distinctive Reformed doctrines? Discuss your answers.

FURTHER STUDY

Sproul, R.C. *Grace Unknown*, pp. 23-40
Sproul, R.C. *Foundations: An Overview of Systematic Theology with R.C. Sproul*
Calvin, John. *Institutes of the Christian Religion*
Luther, Martin. *What Luther Says: An Anthology*

3

Scripture Alone

MESSAGE OVERVIEW

I. *Sola Scriptura* Literally Means "By Scripture Alone"
   a. One question dealt with by the doctrine of *sola Scriptura* relates to the sources of divine revelation, of which there are at least two:
      i. Nature: general revelation
      ii. The Bible: special revelation
   b. The question is whether there is more than one source of special revelation.
   c. According to Protestants, there is only one source of special revelation—Scripture
   d. According to the Roman Catholic Church, there are two sources of special revelation—Scripture and tradition.
   e. At the Council of Trent, Rome declared that the truths of God are found in Scripture and tradition.
   f. There is an ongoing controversy in the Roman church regarding Trent's declaration because of the inherent ambiguity of the Latin terms used.

II. *Sola Scriptura* Also Deals with Questions of Conscience and Controversies
   a. Scripture is the only authority that can bind the conscience.
   b. All controversies over theological questions must be settled in the final analysis by Scripture.

III. *Sola Scriptura* Bears on Questions of Inerrancy
   a. Since Scripture is the Word of God, it is infallible and inerrant.
   b. Some scholars argue that the doctrine of inerrancy was not held by Reformers, but that it was invented by later Reformed "scholastics."
   c. Statements from the Reformers themselves indicate that they believed the Scriptures to be inerrant.

IV. *Sola Scriptura* Involves a Hermeneutical Principle
   a. The Reformers taught the concept of private interpretation—the view that every Christian has the right and responsibility to read and interpret the Bible for himself or herself.
   b. This concept of private interpretation was based on the principle of the perspicuity of Scripture, which means that the basic message of Scripture is plain for any person to see it.

STUDY QUESTIONS

1. What are the two sources of divine revelation and what are the theological terms for these sources?

2. What are the sources of special revelation according to Protestants? According to Rome?

3. How does the doctrine of sola Scriptura bear on theological controversies?

4. What does *sola Scritpura* mean in relation to the conscience?

5. Did the Reformers believe and teach the doctrine of the inerrancy of Scripture?

6. What is the Reformed concept of private interpretation?

7. What is the meaning of "perspicuity"?

DISCUSSION QUESTIONS

1. Discuss the difference between the Protestant and Roman Catholic understandings of the sources of special revelation. Why did the Reformers believe it vital to emphasize Scripture alone as the source of special revelation?

2. What were the Roman Catholic objections to the Protestant principle of private interpretation, and what were their fears? Were the Roman Catholic fears valid? Why or why not?

FURTHER STUDY

Sproul, R.C. *Grace Unknown*, pp. 41-57
Sproul, R.C. *Hath God Said?*
Boice, James Montgomery. *Standing on the Rock: Biblical Authority in a Secular Age*
Kistler, Don, ed. *Sola Scriptura*

4
Faith Alone (Part 1)

MESSAGE OVERVIEW

I. The Doctrine of *Sola Fide* was the Central Controversy of the Protestant Reformation
   a. The Reformers were answering the question of how a person may be found just in the sight of God.
   b. The Reformers did not consider this a debate over trivial issues; instead, they believed it was absolutely crucial.
      i. Martin Luther said the doctrine of *sola fide* is the article upon which the church stands or falls.
      ii. John Calvin said *sola fide* is the hinge upon which everything else in the Christian life turns
   c. Sola fide is a relatively easy doctrine to grasp with the mind, but it is much more difficult to get the doctrine from the head into the heart.
II. The Question—How Can an Unjust Person Survive the Final Judgment of a Just and Holy God?
   a. Romans 3:26—God is both just and the justifier of the one who has faith in Jesus.
   b. When God offers forgiveness, He doesn't just wink at our sin, thereby compromising His holy character.
   c. What man needs is to be justified, and it is God who does the justifying.
III. Justification is Forensic
   a. Justification has to do with a pronouncement in the arena of law.
   b. God justifies us when He declares that He sees us as just.
   c. Justification is a legal declaration by which God declares a person just.
   d. Martin Luther summarized the doctrine with the Latin phrase *simul iustus et peccator*, which means "simultaneously just and sinner".
   e. God pronounces people just while they are still sinners.
   f. Justification by faith alone is theological shorthand for justification by Christ alone.

Faith Alone (Part 1)

g. The fundamental question is this: On the basis of whose righteous does God declare anyone just?

STUDY QUESTIONS

1. What was the central controversy of the Reformation?

2. How did Luther describe the importance of the doctrine of justification by faith alone?

3. Why can God not simply declare everyone forgiven?

4. What is the meaning of the word "forensic"?

5. What is the meaning of the Latin phrase *simul iustus et peccator*?

6. Justification by faith alone is theological shorthand for what?

DISCUSSION QUESTIONS

1. What is the fundamental question dealt with by the doctrine of justification by faith alone, and why is it crucial?

2. Discuss the meaning of forensic justification. Does this doctrine reduce justification to a "legal fiction"?

FURTHER STUDY

Sproul, R.C. *Grace Unknown*, pp. 59-78
Sproul, R.C. *The Cross of Christ*
Sproul, R.C. *Faith Alone*
Buchanan, James. *The Doctrine of Justification*
Kistler, Don, ed. *Justification by Faith Alone*

5

Faith Alone (Part 2)

MESSAGE OVERVIEW

I. The Definition of Justification
   a. Justification is an act by which God declares sinners to be just in His sight.
   b. A problem of definition arose in the medieval church due to the use of the Latin translation of the Bible—the Vulgate.
      i. The word used for justification in the Vulgate was *iustificare*, which means to "make righteous."
      ii. The original Greek word for justification was *diakosune*, which means to reckon a person righteous.
II. The Instrumental Means of Justification—the Roman View
   a. According to the Roman Catholic Church, justification requires faith, but it initially is accomplished through the instrumental cause of baptism.
   b. At baptism, saving grace is infused into the soul, and the person remains in a state of grace unless or until he commits a mortal sin.
   c. After sinning, the person still is said to have faith, but he has lost the grace of justification.
   d. To be restored, the person has to come through what the Council of Trent referred to as the second plank of justification for those who have made shipwreck of their souls—the sacrament of penance.
   e. Penance includes several elements
      i. Sacramental confession
      ii. Priestly absolution
      iii. Works of satisfaction
   f. Works of satisfaction do not provide condign merit—merit that imposes an obligation upon God to bless.
   g. Works of satisfaction produce congruous merit—merit that is real but which rests upon the prior reception of grace and which makes it fitting or congruous of God to restore the person to a state of justification.

Faith Alone (Part 2)

      h. Therefore, according to Rome, the instrumental means of justification is sacramental.

III. The Instrumental Means of Justification—the Reformers' View
- a. The Reformers said the instrumental cause of justification is faith alone.
- b. According to the Reformers, faith is the means by which the righteousness of Christ is given to us.

IV. Infusion vs. Imputation
- a. A central question is: How is the work of Christ appropriated to the sinner?
- b. According to Rome, grace is infused or poured into the soul through the means of sacraments.
- c. The individual Roman Catholic must cooperate with infused grace to the degree that that person actually becomes righteous; then God will declare that person just.
- d. According to the Reformers, the Holy Spirit is infused at the point of regeneration, and God, by means of imputation, justifies those who have faith.
- e. The Reformed doctrine of imputation involves a transfer from one person's account to that of another.
- f. Imputation has two dimensions.
   - i. The Atonement—God imputes the sins of His people to Jesus, who died as a substitute for them, paying the negative penalty of sin.
   - ii. The active obedience of Christ—Christ positively achieved perfect righteousness by perfectly fulfilling God's law, and God imputes that righteousness to the sinner, so that God then sees the sinner under the covering of the righteousness of Christ.
- g. God declares believers just because Christ is just and believers are in Christ by faith.
- h. Martin Luther insisted that the righteousness by which sinners are justified is an alien righteousness, a righteousness that is outside of us.
- i. The good news is that God justifies the ungodly freely by giving them someone else's righteousness—Christ's righteousness, which alone is perfect.

V. The Three Elements of Faith
- a. Notitia—Awareness of the informational content of the Gospel
- b. Assensus—Intellectual assent to the truths of the Gospel
- c. Fiducia—Personal trust and reliance.

VI. Justification and Sanctification
- a. True faith immediately, necessarily, and inevitably will produce the fruit of sanctification.
- b. Faith without works is dead.
- c. According to Luther, true faith is a *fides viva*—a living faith.

STUDY QUESTIONS

1. What is the definition of justification?

2. What is the instrumental means of justification according to the Roman Catholic Church?

3. What are the three elements of the Roman Catholic doctrine of penance?

4. What is the difference between condign merit and congruous merit, according to Rome?

5. What is the instrumental means of justification according to the Reformers?

6. What is the difference between infusion and imputation?

7. What are the two dimensions of imputation?

8. Name and define the three elements of faith.

9. What is the relationship between justification and sanctification?

DISCUSSION QUESTIONS

1. Explain the Roman Catholic doctrine of justification. How does a person become justified in the first place? How does he lose his justification? How can he be restored? Finally, explain what the Reformers saw as fatal to this understanding of justification.

2. There are evangelicals who argue that a Christian may exercise true faith without it ever producing the fruit of sanctification. How does this view square with classical Protestantism? More importantly, how does it fare when measured against Scripture?

FURTHER STUDY

Sproul, R.C. *Grace Unknown*, pp. 59-78
Sproul, R.C. *Getting the Gospel Right*
Sproul, R.C. *Faith Alone*
Buchanan, James. *The Doctrine of Justification*
Kistler, Don, ed. *Justification by Faith Alone*

6

Covenant

MESSAGE OVERVIEW

I. What is Covenant Theology?
   a. Reformed theology sees the structure of the covenant in the Bible as a crucial element in the outworking of the plan of redemption.
   b. For this reason, Reformed theology often is given the nickname "covenant theology."
   c. Reformed theology distinguishes between three chief covenants: the covenant of redemption, the covenant of works, and the covenant of grace.

II. The Covenant of Redemption
   a. The covenant of redemption is a theological concept that refers to the harmony and unity of purpose that has been in existence from all eternity in the mutual relationship and agreement of the three persons of the Trinity.
   b. The Father, Son, and Holy Spirit are all agreed in terms of bringing forth redemption.
   c. There is a difference in function among the members of the Trinity, but no difference in purpose.
      i. Creation and redemption are Trinitarian works.
      ii. The main point of the covenant of redemption as a theological concept is to show the complete agreement that exist within the Trinity.

III. The Covenant of Works
   a. The covenant of works refers to the initial covenant God made with Adam as the representative of all mankind.
   b. God created Adam and Eve and place them in a period of probation, making promises of blessing for obedience and promises of judgment for disobedience.
   c. The destiny of Adam and Eve was determined by their response to God's Law; that is, by their behavior or works—thus, the title "covenant of works."
   d. Because the covenant was made with Adam as the representative of the human race, the whole world is now populated by covenant-breakers.

e. Christ was sent into a world that was guilty.
IV. The Covenant of Grace
   a. Adam and Eve failed under the covenant of works, but God condescended and promised them redemption through a son of Adam.
   b. By this act, God instituted the covenant of grace, which was restated repeatedly to Abraham, Moses, and their descendants.
   c. In the final analysis, the only way any person is justified before God is by works; we are saved by works and by works alone. But whose works?
   d. The covenant of grace must be distinguished from the covenant of works but never separated from it.
   e. It is the covenant of grace that assures us that the covenant of works is finally kept.
   f. The ground of our justification is the perfect work of Christ.
   g. The Second Adam, Jesus submitted to the covenant of works and accomplished what Adam failed to accomplish.
   h. Jesus earned all of the blessing promised originally to Adam.

STUDY QUESTIONS

1. Why is Reformed theology sometimes called covenant theology?

2. Define the covenant of redemption. What is its main point?

3. What is the covenant of works?

4. What is the covenant of grace?

5. In what sense may it be said that we are justified by works and by works alone?

DISCUSSION QUESTIONS

1. Describe some of the similarities and difference between covenant theology and the more popular system of understanding the Bible's structure—dispensationalism.

2. Why is it important that the covenant of works and the covenant of grace not be completely separated?

FURTHER STUDY

Sproul, R.C. *Grace Unknown*, pp. 99-114
Mathison, Keith. *Postmillennialism: An Eschatology of Hope*
Robertson, O. Palmer. *Christ of the Covenants*
Horton, Michael. *Introducing Covenant Theology*

7

Total Depravity (Part 1)

MESSAGE OVERVIEW

I. The Five Points of Calvinism
   a. In the seventeenth century, a theological controversy erupted in the Netherlands between the followers of James Arminius and the Reformed Church.
   b. The Arminian protesters, or Remonstrants, focused on five issues.
   c. The controversy was settled officially at the Synod of Dort, where the Arminian doctrines were condemned and the Reformed doctrines were reaffirmed.
   d. Because the Reformed response followed the manner in which the Arminians protested by affirming five doctrines in particular, these five doctrines have become known as the five points of Calvinism.
   e. They are often remembered through the use of a popular acrostic: TULIP: T (total depravity); U (unconditional election); L (limited atonement); I (irresistible grace); and P (perseverance of the saints).

II. The Pelagian Controversy
   a. If a person understands and embraces the doctrine of total depravity, the other four points will fall into place.
   b. The doctrine first became a matter of controversy during the teaching ministry of Augustine, during what has become known as the Pelagian controversy.
   c. Pelagius protested a statement in a prayer by Augustine: "Command what Thou wouldst, and grant what Thou dost command."
   d. Pelagius objected to the second part, saying that it assumes that the creature is not morally able to do the will of God.
   e. That is exactly the assumption Augustine was making.
   f. At the heart of the controversy was the doctrine of original sin.

III. Original Sin
   a. Original sin does not refer to the first sin; instead, it refers to the consequences of the first sin to the human race.

b. As a result of that first sin, the whole human race fell, and because of that the whole of human nature is influenced by the power of sin.
c. Original sin has to do with the fallen nature of man.
d. Because of the Fall, we are not sinners because we sin; we sin because we are sinners.

IV. The Definition of Total Depravity
   a. Total depravity does not mean utter depravity; it does not mean that every human being is as bad as he or she can be.
   b. Total depravity means that the Fall is so serious that it affects the whole person—body, mind, and will.
   c. The whole person has been infected and corrupted by the power of sin.
   d. The controversy centers on the degree of corruption.

V. Radical Corruption
   a. A better term than total depravity is radical corruption.
   b. Most people believe that man is basically good and that sin is peripheral to his nature.
   c. The Reformed view is that the Fall penetrates to the core of man—to his heart.
   d. Therefore, what is required for man to be conformed to the image of Christ is not simply some small adjustment or behavior modification, but nothing less than renovation from the inside—regeneration by the Holy Spirit.
   e. The only way to escape this radical corruption is for the Holy Spirit to change the core of man.
   f. It must be remembered that even regeneration does not instantly vanquish sin.
   g. The total and final eradication of sin awaits our glorification in heaven.

STUDY QUESTIONS

1. Briefly explain the historical background to the five points of Calvinism.

2. What is the popular acrostic used to remember the five points, and what doctrine does each letter signify?

3. Why did Pelagius object to the prayer of Augustine?

4. What is the definition of original sin?

5. What does total depravity mean? What does it not mean?

6. What is a better term for total depravity?

7. What are the implications of the doctrine of total depravity for our doctrine of regeneration?

DISCUSSION QUESTIONS

1. Does the Reformed doctrine of total depravity accurately describe the nature of fallen man?

2. Why is it important to come to an understanding of the nature of fallen man?

FURTHER STUDY

Sproul, R.C. *Grace Unknown*, pp. 117-137
Sproul, R.C. *A Shattered Image*
Luther, Martin. *The Bondage of the Will*

8

Total Depravity (Part 2)

MESSAGE OVERVIEW

I. The Twofold Debate Over Free Will
   a. One aspect of the debate over free will concerns the relationship between God's sovereignty and our ability to act freely.
   b. The second aspect of the debate over free will concerns the relationship between the Fall and the power of human freedom.
   c. The Westminster Confession of Faith affirms that man has completely lost his freedom in a certain area.
   d. Man has lost the ability to will any spiritual good.

II. The Question of Moral Inability
   a. According to Pelagius, Adam's fall affected only Adam.
   b. The Semi-Pelagian position says that man was affected by Adam's sin in that he is born with a corrupt nature, but there remains a remnant of original righteousness, a power in man's will, that can cooperate with or reject the grace of God.
   c. According to Augustine, the Fall was so profound and the power of sin so strong in man that only God can change the disposition of his soul.
   d. The fundamental issue is whether fallen man has the moral power to incline himself to God's offers of help, or whether God must do an initial work of re-creation in the soul before the person has the moral power to say yes to the Gospel.

III. The Divine Initiative
   a. Before a person comes to Christ, God works unilaterally, monergistically, independently, and sovereignly by changing the soul of the sinner, which is by nature dead in sin and morally unable to resurrect itself.
   b. God has to give a person new spiritual life before that person has the power to come to Christ.

IV. Monergistic Regeneration
   a. Regeneration is a work of God alone.

Total Depravity (Part 2)

      b. This work rests upon grace alone, and there is nothing a man can do to earn it or merit it.
      c. Jesus says in John 6:63ff, "No one can come to me unless it has been granted to him by My Father."
      d. "No man" is a universal negative proposition—it says something negative about everybody.
      e. "Can" means ability or power—no man has the ability or power to do the task in question.
      f. "Come to me" means to embrace Christ in faith—this is what no man has the ability or power to do.
      g. "Unless" points to a necessary condition that must be met before a desired situation is realized.
      h. "It is granted to him by My Father" is the necessary condition—God has to enable a person to come to Christ.
      i. Man has lost the natural ability to come to Christ.

V. The Bondage of the Will
      a. Man still makes choices, but only according to his desires.
      b. The very essence of freedom is the ability to choose according to our desires.
      c. The problem is moral bondage.
      d. We are slaves to our own desires.
      e. By nature we have no desire for Christ or the things of God.
      f. We freely reject God unless God changes the desires of our hearts.

STUDY QUESTIONS

1. What are the two aspects of the debate over free will?

2. What is the Pelagian understanding of moral ability? The Semi-Pelagian? The Augustinian?

3. What is the fundamental issue at stake in the debate over moral inability?

4. What is meant by the term "the Divine Initiative"?

5. What is the meaning of monergistic?

6. What is the relationship between man's desires and his will?

DISCUSSION QUESTIONS

1. What are some of the primary strengths of the Reformed Augustinian doctrine of total depravity? Are there any weaknesses? Discuss your answers.

2. Read John 6:63ff and discuss the exegesis of this passage found in the lecture. How does this verse inform our doctrine of total depravity? What other verses shed light on this subject?

FURTHER STUDY

Edwards, Jonathan. *Freedom of the Will*
Sproul, R.C. *Grace Unknown*, pp. 117-137
Luther, Martin. *The Bondage of Will*

9

Unconditional Election

MESSAGE OVERVIEW

I. A Definition of Unconditional Election
   a. Unconditional election does not mean that God saves people whether they believe in Christ or not.
   b. The question is this: On what basis does God elect to save certain people?
   c. Conditional election teaches that God elects on the basis of His foreknowledge; He foresees who will have faith and elects them unto salvation.
   d. Unconditional election insists that God's elective decree rests solely on His sovereign decision to save whom He will; there is no foreseen condition that people meet, thereby inducing God to elect them.

II. Romans 9
   a. In Romans 9, the apostle Paul gives an exposition of the doctrine of election by providing an illustration from the Old Testament; the story of Jacob and Esau.
   b. He explains that the purposes of God are the foundation for His choices.
   c. In verse 14, he raises and answers an anticipated objection: "Is there unrighteousness with God? Certainly not."
   d. If Paul were teaching the Arminian or Semi-Pelagian view, who would raise any objection about unfairness?
   e. Reformed theology hears the same objection Paul heard.
   f. In verse 15, Paul writes that God will have mercy on whom He will have mercy.
   g. It is God's divine right to execute clemency when and upon whom He so desires.
   h. If God chooses to give grace to some and not to others, there is no violation of justice—one group receives grace, the other receives justice.
   i. Salvation is based upon free will—the free will of a sovereign God.

STUDY QUESTIONS

1. What is the meaning of unconditional election?

2. What does unconditional election not mean?

3. What is the definition of conditional election?

4. What objection does Paul anticipate to his doctrine of election as explained in Romans 9?

5. Is there a violation of justice if God give grace only to some? Explain.

DISCUSSION QUESTIONS

1. Many Arminians believe that conditional election solves all of the difficulties in relating God's sovereignty and man's free will. Examine this idea by discussing the following question: If God foresees a human act of faith before the foundation of the world and elects that person on that basis, is that person free to not choose God? What are the implications of the answer for one's understanding of God's omniscience?

2. In your opinion, can Paul's teaching in Romans 9 be reconciled with any doctrine other than unconditional election? If so, how would the objection Paul anticipates retain its relevance?

FURTHER STUDY

Sproul, R.C. *Grace Unknown*, pp. 139-161
Sproul, R.C. *Chosen by God*

10

Limited Atonement

MESSAGE OVERVIEW

I. A Definition of Limited Atonement
   a. Limited atonement is the most controversial of the five points of Calvinism.
   b. Limited atonement does not mean that there is a limit to the value or merit of Christ's atonement.
   c. Christ's atonement is sufficient for all, and anyone who trusts Christ will receive the full measure of the benefits of that atonement.
   d. The doctrine of limited atonement is concerned with the original purpose, design, and plan of God in sending Christ to die on the cross.
   e. The question is whether it was God's intent to make salvation possible for everyone, allowing for the possibility that it would be effective for no one (unlimited atonement), or whether God, from all eternity, had a plan of salvation by which He designed the atonement to ensure the salvation of His people.
   f. A better term is definite redemption; it communicates that God designed the work of redemption specifically with a view to providing salvation for the elect.

II. God is Not Willing That Any Should Perish
   a. There are many objections raised against the doctrine of limited atonement, all of which are answered in great detail by John Owen in his book *The Death of Death in the Death of Christ*.
   b. Here, we will focus on one particular objection that is based upon one reading of 2 Peter 3:8ff, where Peter says, "The Lord is... not willing that any should perish but that all should come to repentance."
   c. The problem centers on the understanding of two words in the text: "willing" and "any."

III. Uses of the Word "Will" in Scripture
   a. The decretive will of God is that will by which God brings to pass whatsoever He decrees; if Peter is using "willing" in this sense, this is a perfect proof text for universalism, because it teaches that no one will perish.
   b. The preceptive will of God involves the commands God gives His people, commands that people violate. It is unlikely that Peter is saying that it is a violation of God's law for someone to perish.
   c. God's will of disposition involves that which pleases God, His disposition. Peter probably is using "willing" in this sense.
IV. The Meaning of "Any"
   a. If "any" means all human beings, then "willing" can mean only the disposition of God.
   b. But in this context, "any" may not mean "any human being."
   c. In verse 9, Peter says that God is "longsuffering toward us, not willing that any should perish."
   d. The immediate antecedent of "any" is "us."
   e. The context indicates that "us" is reference to believers in Christ.

STUDY QUESTIONS

1. What is the definition of limited atonement?

2. What is the primary concern of the doctrine of limited atonement?

3. What is the definition of unlimited atonement?

4. What is the decretive will of God?

5. What is the preceptive will of God?

6. What is God's will of disposition?

7. What are some of the possible interpretations of 2 Peter 3:8ff?

DISCUSSION QUESTIONS

1. Unlimited atonement teaches that Christ died to make salvation possible for all men. Does Scripture teach that Christ died to make salvation possible or that He died to save? Provide scriptural examples.

2. If Scripture teaches that Christ died to save rather than merely to make salvation possible, why is it scripturally impossible to say that Christ died for all men?

3. What passages of Scripture are most difficult to reconcile with the doctrine of unlimited atonement? With limited atonement? Which doctrine provides the best explanation of all the relevant passages? Discuss your answers.

FURTHER STUDY

Sproul, R.C. *Grace Unknown*, pp. 163-177
Owen, John. *The Death of Death in the Death of Christ.*

11

Irresistible Grace

MESSAGE OVERVIEW

I. A Definition of Irresistible Grace
   a. Irresistible grace conjures up the idea that no one can resist the grace of God, but the history of man is a history of resistance to God's grace.
   b. A better term for irresistible grace is effectual grace.
   c. The idea of effectual grace is that the grace of God is so powerful it can overcome our natural resistance to it.
   d. Effectual grace means that saving grace effects what God intends to effect by it.

II. Faith and Regeneration
   a. At issue in this concept is the relationship between faith and regeneration.
   b. If there is any one point that divides Reformed theology from another theology historically, it is the question of the relation between faith and regeneration.
   c. According to Reformed theology, regeneration precedes faith—not chronologically in time but logically in terms of necessary priority.
   d. The most common view today is that faith causes regeneration; in other words, if you believe you will be born again.
   e. This Semi-Pelagian view assumes that man still has the natural ability to believe if God draws him.
   f. It is evident at this point that the resolution of the problem will depend on how total depravity is understood.
   g. Jesus tells us that no man can come to Him unless it is given to Him by the Father.
   h. In Ephesians 2:1ff, Paul tells us that we were dead in trespasses and sins, that God made us alive, and that faith is a gift of God.

III. Regeneration
   a. Regeneration is spiritual resurrection accomplished by God.

b. The Holy Spirit doesn't drag a person kicking and screaming against his will into the kingdom; instead, He changes the inclination and disposition of the heart so that the person is willing to embrace Christ.
c. A man comes to Christ because he wants to come to Christ, but he only wants to come to Christ because God already has done a work of grace in his soul.
d. Without the prior work of God in the soul, the person never will want to come to Christ.
e. Regeneration is monergistic; it is the work of God alone because He alone has the power to change the disposition of the heart.

STUDY QUESTIONS

1. Why is the term irresistible grace confusing and misleading?

2. What is the meaning of effectual grace?

3. What is the key point at issue in the doctrine of effectual grace?

4. When Reformed theology says regeneration precedes faith, what is meant by the term "precedes"?

5. What is the most common position today regarding the relationship between regeneration and faith?

6. What is the meaning of regeneration?

7. Does anyone come to Christ who does not want to?

DISCUSSION QUESTIONS

1. Explain how a person's understanding of total depravity will determine his understanding of effectual grace, if he is consistent.

2. What does the metaphor of spiritual resurrection and spiritual birth reveal about the nature of regeneration, specifically as it relates to man's cooperation in the accomplishment of the work?

FURTHER STUDY

Sproul, R.C. *Grace Unknown*, pp. 179-196
Sproul, R.C. *The Mystery of the Holy Spirit*
Sproul, R.C. *The Holy Spirit*
Ferguson, Sinclair. *The Holy Spirit*

12

Perseverance of the Saints

MESSAGE OVERVIEW

I. A Definition of Perseverance of the Saints
   a. The term perseverance presents us with difficulties because it suggests that it is something we do in and of ourselves.
   b. A better term for this doctrine is preservation of the saints, because the preservation is accomplished by God.
   c. The preservation of the saints means that all who have been elected by the Father, atoned for by Christ, and regenerated by the Holy Spirit will be saved for all of eternity, and that not one of them will fall away totally or finally.

II. The Foundation of the Doctrine of Preservation
   a. What God starts he will finish. Philippians 1:6 says, "He who has begun a good work in you will complete it until the day of Jesus Christ."
   b. If you have it, you never will lose it; if you lost it, you never had it. 1 John 2:19 says, "They went out from us, but they were not of us; for if they had been of us, they would have continued with us."
   c. In Matthew 7:23, Jesus says He will say to some of those who call Him Lord, "I never knew you; depart from me."
   d. In John 17:12, Jesus thanks the Father that all who have been given to Him are saved.

III. Christians and Sin
   a. Even after being saved, Christians can lapse into serious sin.
   b. David was a regenerate man, a man after God's own heart, but he committed adultery and conspiracy to murder.
   c. Peter rejected Jesus Christ publicly and with oaths.
   d. True Christians can have radical and serious falls, but not total and final falls.
   e. Church discipline is to be done with a view towards repentance.
   f. Our judgment toward those who have professed Christ and have fallen should be a judgment of charity.

IV. The Holy Spirit and Preservation
   a. The Holy Spirit who raises us from spiritual death also raises us unto eternal life.
   b. The Holy Spirit not only initiates the work of salvation, He preserves it.
   c. We have the Holy Spirit as an earnest, a down payment.
   d. We are sealed by the Spirit for eternity.
V. The Intercession of Christ
   a. One of the main reasons Christians can have confidence is the ongoing intercessory work of Christ.
   b. He is our Great High Priest, who intercedes for us daily.

STUDY QUESTIONS

1. What is the definition of the preservation of the saints?

2. What are some of the Scripture texts that teach this doctrine?

3. Can Christians commit sin? Serious sin? The unforgivable sin?

4. Provide some biblical examples of believers who fell into serious sin.

5. What should be our judgment toward those who profess Christ and fall into serious sin?

6. How does the Holy Spirit work for the preservation of the saints?

7. What aspect of Christ's work gives us confidence in the preservation of the saints?

DISCUSSION QUESTIONS

1. How important is the doctrine of the preservation of the saints to a Christian's walk with God?

2. Explain why, if one accepts the first four points of Calvinism, the preservation of the saints follows. Why would the preservation of the saints be an impossible doctrine to maintain consistently if a person rejected one or more of the first four points.

FURTHER STUDIES

Sproul, R.C. *Grace Unknown*, pp. 197-216
Sproul, R.C. *Dust to Glory: An Overview of the Bible with R.C. Sproul*
The Heidelberg Catechism
Gerstner, John. *The Westminster Confession of Faith*